COAL & COKE
1

The Reverend W. Awdry's Railway Series

RAILWAY MAP

A full colour, laminated map showing where Thomas the Tank Engine and his friends live and work. Designed by Peter Edwards, it shows the layout of the Fat and Thin Controllers' Railways on the Island of Sodor. When open it measures 21 × 33½ in. (50p net).

SURPRISE PACKET

Designed and drawn by Peter Edwards, the Reverend W. Awdry's *Surprise Packet* is full of stories, games, puzzles, things to make and things to do (11½ × 11½ in., 12 sheets printed in full colour and black-and-white, and bound into a laminated portfolio, 90p net).

RECORDS

Johnny Morris tells the first 32 stories (books 1–4) on 4 L.P. records (*The Railway Stories Vols 1–4* in "The World of Children's Stories" series), obtainable from the Decca Record Company Ltd.

PUZZLES

Eight puzzles featuring Thomas the Tank Engine and his friends are now available from Whitman Publishing (U.K.) Ltd. Each puzzle is printed in full colour, made up of 30 large wooden pieces, and measures approximately 8¾ × 6⅝ in.

Railway Series, No. 23

ENTERPRISING ENGINES

by

THE REV. W. AWDRY

with illustrations by

GUNVOR & PETER EDWARDS

KAYE & WARD LIMITED

21 NEW STREET, LONDON, EC2M 4NT

First published by Kaye & Ward Ltd
21 New Street, London EC2M 4NT
1968
Reprinted 1973
First reprinted in paperback form 1973

ISBN 0 7182 0432 8

Printed in England by Jarrold & Sons Ltd, Norwich

DEAR RICHARD,

Do you remember the photographs you took of what happened to your train on the way to Waterloo in April 1967?

Your Mother, very kindly, gave me a set, and they helped our artist to draw at least two of the pictures for "Super Rescue".

Anyway, "Super Rescue" is the story which your pictures told me. I hope you will enjoy it, and the other three stories as well.

THE AUTHOR

The author gratefully acknowledges the ready help given by *Flying Scotsman*'s owner, Mr. A. F. PEGLER, and his assistant, Mr. E. HOYLE, in the preparation of this book.

Tenders for Henry

"I'm not happy," complained Gordon.

"Your fire-box is out of order," said James. "No wonder, after all that coal you had yesterday."

"Hard work brings good appetite," snapped Gordon. "*You* wouldn't understand."

"I know," put in Duck, brightly. "It's boiler-ache. I warned you about that standpipe on the Other Railway; but you drank gallons."

"It's *not* boiler-ache," protested Gordon. "It's . . . ."

"Of course it is," said Henry. "That water's bad. It furs up your tubes. Your boiler must be full of sludge. Have a good wash-out. Then, you'll feel a different engine."

"Don't be vulgar," said Gordon huffily.

Gordon backed down on his train, hissing mournfully.

"Cheer up, Gordon!" said the Fat Controller.

"I can't, Sir. The others say I've got boiler-ache, but I haven't, Sir. I keep thinking about the Dreadful State of the World, Sir. Is it true, Sir, what the diesels say?"

"What do they say?"

"They boast that they've *abolished Steam*, Sir."

"Yes, Gordon. It is true."

"What, Sir! All my Doncaster brothers, drawn the same time as me?"

"All gone, except one."

The Guard's whistle blew, and Gordon puffed sadly away.

SUNNY

"Poor old Gordon!" said the Fat Controller. "Hmm . . . . If only we could! . . . Yes, I'll ask his Owner at once." He hurried away.

Arrangements took time, but one evening, Gordon's Driver ran back, excited. "Wake up, Gordon! The Fat Controller's given you a surprise. Look!"

Gordon could hardly believe it. Backing towards him were two massive green tenders, and their engine's shape was very like his own. "It's Flying Scotsman!" he gasped. "The Fat Controller's brought him to see me. Oh thank you, Sir!"

Gordon's toot of joy was drowned by Flying Scotsman's as he drew happily alongside.

LNER
4472

Next day the two engines were photographed side by side.

"You've changed a lot," smiled Flying Scotsman.

"I had a 'rebuild' at Crewe. They didn't do a proper Doncaster job, of course, but it serves."

"I had a 'rebuild' too, and looked hideous. But my Owner said I was an Extra Special Engine, and made them give me back my proper shape."

"Is that why you have two tenders, being Special?"

"No. You'd hardly believe it, Gordon, but Over There, they've hardly *any coal and water*."

"But surely, every *proper* railway . . . ."

"Exactly. You are lucky, Gordon, to have a Controller who knows how to run railways."

FLYING

Everyone got on well with Flying Scotsman except Henry. Henry was jealous.

"Tenders are marks of distinction," he complained. "Everybody knows that. Why's he got two?"

"He's famous," explained Duck and Donald. "He was the second to go 100 miles an hour; besides, the Other Railway has no coal and water."

"Pooh!" sniffed Henry. "I can't believe *that*! I never boast," he continued, "but I always work hard enough for two. I deserve another tender for that."

Duck whispered something to Donald.

"Henry," asked Duck innocently, "would you like *my* tenders?"

"Yours!" exclaimed Henry. "What have *you* got to do with tenders?"

"All right," said Duck. "The deal's off. Would you like them Donald?"

"I wudna deprive ye of the honour."

"It *is* a great honour," said Duck, thoughtfully, "but I'm only a tank-engine, so I don't really understand tenders. Perhaps James might . . . ."

"I'm sorry I was rude," said Henry hastily. "How many tenders have you, and when could I have them?"

"Six, and you can have them this evening."

"Six lovely tenders," chortled Henry. "What a splendid sight I'll be! That'll show the others the sort of engine I am!"

G
DONALD

Henry was excited. "D'you think it'll be all right?" he asked for the umpteenth time.

"Of course," said Duck. "Just go where I told you, and they'll all be ready."

Meanwhile, word had gone round, and the others waited where they could get a good view. Henry was cheered to the echo when he came, but he wasn't a splendid sight. He had six tenders, true, but they were very old and very dirty. All were filled with boiler sludge!

"Had a good wash-out, Henry?" called a voice. "That's right. You feel a different engine now." Henry was not sure, but he thought the voice was Gordon's.

4472
LNER

Super Rescue

THE two diesels surveyed the shed. "It's time, 7101," said one, "that we took this railway over."

"Shsh, 199! It's *their* railway, after all."

"Not for long," persisted 199. "Our Controller says, 'Steam engines spoil our Image'."

"Of course we do," snapped Duck. "We show what frauds you are. Call yourselves engines? If anything happens, *you* care nothing for your train. *You* just moan for a fitter. *We* bring it home, if only on one cylinder."

"Nothing," boasted 199, "*ever* happens to us. *We* are reliable."

Vulgar noises greeted this.

"How rude!" said 199.

"You asked for it," growled 7101. "Now shut up!"

G W

Next day, Henry was rolling home, tender-first. "I'm a 'failed engine'," he mourned. "Lost my Regulator—Driver says it's jammed wide open, and he can't mend it till I'm cool."

"However," he went on, "I've got steam, and Driver can use my Reverser; but it *would* happen after Duck fooled me with those tenders. Now they'll laugh at me again."

He reached a signalbox and stopped, whistling for a "road".

Opposite the Box, on the "up" line, stood diesel 199 with a train of oil-tankers.

"Worse and worse," thought Henry. "Now 'Old Reliable' will laugh at me, too."

D199

The Signalman came out. "For pity's sake take this Spamcan away. It's failed. The 'Limited' is behind, and all he does is wail for his Fitter."

"Spamcan!" fumed 199. "I'm . . . ."

"Stow it!" snapped the Signalman, "or I'll take my tin-opener to you. Now then!"

199 subsided at this dreadful threat, and Henry pulled the train out of the way. The diesel didn't help. He just sulked.

The "Limited" rushed by with a growl and a roar. Henry gave a chuckle. "Look, Spamcan," he said. "There's your little pal."

The diesel said nothing. He hoped 7101 hadn't noticed.

3

7101 hadn't noticed. He had troubles of his own. He was cross with his coaches. They seemed to be getting heavier. He roared at them, but it did no good.

Engines have a pump called an Ejector, which draws air out of the train's brake pipes to keep the brakes "off". If it fails, air leaks in and the brakes come "on", gently at first, then harder and harder.

7101's Ejector had failed. The brakes were already "leaking on" while he passed Henry. He struggled on for half a mile before being brought to a stand, growling furiously, unable to move a wheel.

3
D199

"Well! Well! Well! Did you hear what Signalman said?"

"I thought they'd be laughing at me!" chuckled Henry. "Now, the joke's on them!"

"Moving two 'dead' diesels and their trains?" said his Driver thoughtfully. "That's no joke for a 'failed' engine. D'you think you can do it?"

"I'll have a good try," said Henry with spirit. "Anyway, 7101's better than old Spam-can. He did try and shut him up last night."

"Come on, then," said his Driver. "We mustn't keep the passengers waiting."

"GET MOV – ING YOU!" Henry puffed the sulky diesel into motion, and started to the rescue.

Henry gently buffered up to the express. While the two Drivers talked, his Fireman joined his front brake-pipe to the coaches.

"It's better than we thought, Henry," said his Driver. "The diesel can pull if we keep the brakes 'off'. So the only weight we'll have is Spamcan's goods."

"Whoosh!" said Henry. "That's a mercy." He was, by now, feeling rather puffed.

"Poop poop poopoop! Are you ready?" tooted 7101.

"Peep peep peeeep! Yes I am!" whistled Henry.

So, with 7101 growling in front, and Henry gamely puffing in the middle, the long cavalcade set out for the next Big Station.

Donald and Flying Scotsman were waiting. They cheered as Henry puffed past.

He braked the coaches thankfully; Spamcan and the tankers trailed far behind.

The passengers buzzed out like angry bees; but the Fat Controller told them about Henry, so they forgot to be cross and thanked Henry instead. They called him an Enterprising Engine, and took his photograph.

They were thrilled too, when Flying Scotsman backed down on their train. If the Guard hadn't tactfully "shooed" them to their coaches the train would have started later than ever.

Donald took the "goods". "Return 199 to the Other Railway," ordered the Fat Controller. "I will write my views later."

Henry and 7101 went away together.

"I'm sorry about last night," ventured the diesel.

"That's all right. You did shut 'Old Reliable' up."

"And," said the diesel ruefully, "made a fool of myself today too."

"Rubbish! A failed Ejector might happen to anyone: I'd lost my Regulator."

"You! Failed?" exclaimed the diesel. "And yet . . . ." His voice trailed away in admiration.

"Well!" said Henry. "Emergency, you know. Trains *must* get through."

7101 said no more. He had a lot to think about.

7101

Escape

DOUGLAS had taken the "Midnight Goods" to a station on the Other Railway. He was shunting ready for his return journey, when he heard a faint "Hisssssssssssss".

"That sounds like an engine," he thought.

The "Hisssss" came again. This time, it sounded almost despairing. "Who's there?" he asked.

A whisper came. "Are you a Fat Controller's engine?"

"Aye, and proud of it."

"Thank goodness! I'm Oliver. We're escaping to your railway, but we've run out of coal, and I've no more steam."

"Is it from scrap ye're escaping?"

"Yes."

"Then it's glad I'll be to help ye; but we maun wurrk fast."

Both crews joined in. They took off Oliver's side-rods, wrote out transit labels, and chalked SCRAP everywhere they could. Douglas marshalled Oliver in front of his train. "No time to turrn round," he panted. "I maun run tender furrst."

"Yoohoo! Yoohoo!" yelled a passing diesel. "A steamer's escaping! Yoohoo!"

Douglas puffed firmly on. "Take no notice," he counselled; but they were stopped before they could clear the station throat.

SCRAP
SCRAP

The Foreman's lamp shone on Oliver. "Aha!" he exclaimed. "A 'Western' engine!" His light flickered further back. "A 'Western' auto-coach, and goods-brake too! You can't take these."

"Can we no!" said Douglas' Driver. "They're all fer uz. See fer yeself."

Douglas' Guard showed him the labels and papers. Oliver's crew, hiding in the coach, hardly dared to breathe.

"Seems in order," said the Foreman grudgingly, "but it's queer."

"Sure, and it is," began the Guard, "but I could tell you queerer . . . ."

"So could I!" interrupted the Foreman. "Right away, Guard."

"A near thing," puffed Douglas with relief.

"We've had worse," smiled Oliver. "We ran at night. Friendly signalmen would pass us from box to box when no trains were about. We got on well till 'Control' heard about a 'mystery train'. Then, they tried to hunt us down."

"What did you do?"

"A signalman let us hide on an old quarry branch. Driver, Fireman and Guard blocked the cutting with rubbish, and levered one of the approach rails away. We stayed there for days, with diesels baying and growling like hounds outside. I was very frightened then."

"Small blame to you," said Douglas feelingly.

Presently they rumbled over the bridge and on to the Fat Controller's Railway.

"We're home! They can't catch ye noo."

"Tell Isabel and Toad please."

Douglas called out the news, and heard a joyful "Tingalingaling! Tingalingaling!" He was surprised.

Oliver chuckled. "That's Isabel," he said. "There is a bell on her you see. She's clever. When we go out together, I pull one way, and push the other. When I pull, I can see ahead. When I push, I can't; so Isabel keeps a good look-out, and rings her bell to talk to me."

"Ye dinna say!" Douglas was impressed.

'Aboot this Toad," he continued. "Is he. . . ."

"Haud yer wheesht," said his Driver. "Yon's the Wurrks. We maun slip in unbeknownst, and find a place for Oliver."

Douglas tried hard to be quiet, but the Night Foreman heard them, and had to be told their secret. "I know just the place," he said, and showed them an empty siding nicely hidden away.

Oliver said "Goodbye" and "Thank you", and Douglas puffed away. "Yon's an enterprising engine," he thought. "I won away here with Donald; but I'd've been feared to do it on my own."

Little Western

DOUGLAS arrived back in time to see Flying Scotsman take his Enthusiasts home.

The Fat Controller said they had all been honoured, and thanked Flying Scotsman and his Owner for their help. "Please tell everyone," he went on, "that whatever happens elsewhere, steam will still be at work here. We shall be glad to welcome all who want to see, and travel behind, *real* engines."

This announcement was greeted with cheers, and Flying Scotsman departed to the strains of "Will ye no come back again?" led, as one might expect, by Donald and Douglas.

At last Douglas could tell his news. They were all excited about it, and agreed that something must be done for Oliver.

"I'm feared," said Donald, "some murdering diesel may creep in, and him there alone, lacking steam even to whistle for help."

"You're right," said James. "He won't be safe till the Fat Controller knows."

"Douglas should tell him at once," said Gordon firmly.

"Is it me speak to the Fat Controller? It's forward he'd think me, and maybe interfering."

"Well, here he is!" said a cheerful voice. "Now, what's this all about?"

Duck broke the awkward silence. "Beg pardon, Sir, but we do need another engine."

"I agree, Duck. That is why I am giving 7101 another chance." Their faces showed such dismay that the Fat Controller had difficulty with his own!

"Sir," ventured Gordon at last. "We had hoped for a *real* engine."

"They," said the Fat Controller gravely, "are rare, and unless one escapes, there's little hope . . . ."

"But, Sirr," burst out Donald, "one *has* . . ."

". . . and, thanks to Douglas, is now at our Works," announced the Fat Controller.

"Sirr," gasped Douglas, "Is there anything ye don't know?"

"More than you think," he laughed.

"Oliver's crew told me all you did, Douglas . . . ."

"Och, Sirr! Ye couldna' see a braw wee engine, and him in trouble, and no do a wheel's turn . . . ."

"More than 'a wheel's turn', I fancy. Douglas, I'm pleased with you. Oliver, Isabel, and Toad will soon be ours. Oliver and Isabel are just what we need for Duck's Branch Line . . . ."

Loud cheers greeted this announcement.

". . . and Toad wants to be your brakevan, Douglas."

"Thank you, Sirr. I'd hoped for that. He and I'll do brawly together."

G W R

That, of course, made everything right. Henry spoke a good word for 7101, and the others gave him a welcome.

He had good manners for a start, so Henry didn't find it hard to teach him our ways. 7101 finds them different from those of the Other Railway, but much more interesting. He is now quite a useful engine.

They teased him at first because of his growls. They said he was like a bear. He still growls, not because he is cross, but because he can't help it. His name, "Bear", has stuck. He likes it.

"It's nicer than just a number," he says. "Having a name means that you really belong."

D5

The Fat Controller soon had Oliver, Isabel, and Toad mended and painted in full Great Western colours. Then, he rescued three more "Western" auto-coaches. Two, Alice and Mirabel, he gave to Duck. The third, Dulcie, joined Oliver and Isabel.

Duck and Oliver are happy on their Branch Line. It runs along the coast to the Small Railway. "We *re-open* Branches," they boast.

They are very proud of this indeed.

The others laughed at first, and called their Branch "The Little Western". Duck and Oliver were delighted, and now, no one ever thinks of calling it anything else.

COAL & COKE
1